praise for TWENTY-ONE FAREWELLS

In this series of farewells, both common and profound, Emily Kerlin explores the complex relationships—with parents, lovers, children, and animals both wild and domestic—that make us human. These poems sing with the details of a life full of grief and joy, from the "acrid, eggy smoke" of Fourth of July fireworks to a bat swooping through a church "like a small, leathery kite," and uncover moments of beauty even in places where "death swims / close to the surface." Here you will find hawks and house fires, illness and hope, ocean breezes and heart-wrenching goodbyes. Like the women she so lovingly describes in "The Great Grandmothers," Kerlin's poems are tough, tender, and "lovely, even in their fear."

> —Mark Neely, author of *Four of a Kind, Beasts of the Hill, Dirty Bomb* and *Ticker*

The *Twenty-One Farewells* are ballads of loss and love--tiny portraitures of families in and out of marriage, apartments, and life. In kitchens and fields and roads, Kerlin creates landscapes where even the clouds above, "race past,/as if there was someplace else to be," and comfort down below comes in the form of sweet charred fruit spooned "into our mouths like we are/our own mothers." It's a heart-wrenching and thought-provoking first collection.

> —Gale Walden, author of *Same Blue Chevy* and *Where The Time Goes*

In poems salted with honesty and leavened with compassion, Emily Kerlin says farewell to an alcoholic "cutest cousin," to youthful suicides, to a drowned tabby, an injured dog taken to the burn pit, a childhood home burning before her eyes. She says farewell to lost innocence, pre-Covid normality, a daughter moving into her first apartment, first marriages, her own and others'. She ponders how we might say farewell to a planet careening toward catastrophe. And having created in precise and graceful language this world of loss, she says farewell to despair and loneliness. She shows us that, like crocuses emerging into a cold March morning, we, too, can push through, vibrantly alive even in our fear. Pack these poems in your survival kit.

—*John Palen,* author of *Open Communion: New and Selected Poems, Distant Music* and *Riding With the Diaspora*

In her moving debut book of poetry, Emily Kerlin asks, "Have you ever loved / anything more" than being alone in this world of "loon calling"? Her tender and empathetic voice draws us into blended families, lifelong partners, a bat trapped in a church as "a small leathery kite," or part of a blue towel on a creek's rocky bank, "waving in the icy water / covering and uncovering the tender shape / of a tabby, its fur like the flash of a shy fish." Within this world, she gives us an intimacy of disruption/intrusion and an ending in which a person begins anew, as when she checks on her neighbor-widower from the sidewalk and observes, "light peers over / his softly sloping shoulders." In the end, *Twenty-One Farewells* is about the redeeming values of intimate observation and connection within a sense of isolation or loss.

—*Robert Manaster,* the co-author of a translation of Ronny Someck's *The Milk Underground*

Twenty-One Farewells is a meditation on loss in its many forms: loss of earlier selves, of childhood innocence; loss in nature, in the death of animals both wild and domestic; loss of trust, home, expectation, connection. In spare, vivid vignettes, the poems in this collection switch subjects deftly, each guided by a clear-eyed, compassionate observer who unflinchingly mines the place "where loss lives in the chest." *Twenty-One Farewells* speaks to grief, suicide, addiction, and illness in a language of both clarity and empathy, while also moving beyond mere lamentation. For while some poems explore the kind of grief that comes unbidden—unstoppable as the hawk's snatch—others challenge us to consider our own role in inflicting loss, to acknowledge that human tendency to "set / small fires that we presume / to know how to extinguish." Reading this collection, I found space for both sorrow and hope, space to hold the paradoxical truth that, like the speaker, although "the things I love / are too many and far / too difficult to carry," the beauty within that struggle can also be "more than enough."

—Emily Patterson, contest judge

twenty-one farewells

emily f. kerlin

MINERVA RISING PRESS
Boca Raton

Cover art by Jason Michael Bentley
Book design by Brooke Schultz

ISBN 978-1-950811-21-2

Printed and bound in USA
First Printing February 2024

Published by Minerva Rising Press
17717 Circle Pond Ct
Boca Raton, FL 33496

contents

No single thing abides; but all things flow.
Fragment to fragment clings-the things thus grow
Until we know and name them. By degrees
They melt, and are no more the things we know.

—Lucretius

Fourth of July

This time we're close enough
to taste the acrid, eggy smoke.

You ask about constellations
and planets, then pull up an app,
find Venus, the one that pops
out like a celestial punch
from the busy black above us.

I think you like sitting here,
with your mom on one side and your dad
on the other, even though the wide lens
has a stepmother and stepfather
flanking our row of folding chairs.

You have a lot of questions,
but not about the days when things were
different. What would be the point?
Even a twelve-year-old knows
where loss lives in the chest.

You ask instead why the satellites
and arcing fireworks don't collide.
Why airplanes overhead
don't ignite as they blink by.
And the answer, of course,
is that some things that appear
close are, in fact, very far apart.

Bucks

My father-in-law quickly calls
the neighbors, who come to gawk

as they wrestle like hooked boats
in the savage waves of a storm,

black eyes wild with panic.
Air spasms with snorts,

the hollow clashes of their twisted-up
tines and long, guttural moans.

One man, giggling like a boy,
stops briefly to take stock, then cocks

his rifle and after two swift pops
they fall with a final clatter.

Red pools form as the bucks shiver
into their sleep and we hush, too,

while above us white clouds race past,
as if there was someplace else to be.

.

emily f. kerlin

The Golden Boy Goes on Hospice

Wasn't it June
when we met in Wrigleyville
and sat outside, so the sun
could kiss you, the cutest
of all the cousins?
I thought you were sober
but you ordered the house red.
Your eyes laughed,
two bright cerulean bays.

By February the blond curls
are clipped, skin clings
to cheek and jaw,
urine-yellow
or cadaver-gray,
depending on the light.
Your eyes are dark
lagoons and death swims
close to the surface.
Your gums bleed.
Your mouth is open but
through with the work
of words.

I was thinking about that day
on the patio, how we joked

about the Cubs and the pigeons,
then laughed about how angry
grandpa would get when we ran
into the September corn.
The first place you knew of
where you could get so lost
you might never be found.

Christmas Eve

It was the third verse, just as our mouths fixed
triumphant. Our eyes shifted from the brown

hymnal to heaven as he prepared his second
liftoff from the choir loft, swooping down

like a small, leathery kite. This time he pinged
his ultrasonic notes to the altar. The woman

of the cloth ducked. We sang on with trepidation
to Bethlehem as he took flight again. Hands covered

heads. The air flashed with frantic light. Windows
opened to the night. The nave turned cold. Glory

in the highest trailed as he winged his panicked
body into the pipes of a 1912 Kilgan & Son.

It rang out loudly for the Lord, and we promised
to adore Him before all went quiet. A woman rose

to close the window. A girl in a red satin dress
stood in the aisle, head tipped back. Eyes wide.

Night Shift

You read crop reports
until the furnace quiets
at midnight, then close
your eyes and lean into
the old armchair.

Scout follows your boy
out the door, across
the field to the barn.
He returns alone,
barking, around one.

You will walk out there
in your boots and robe,
Hail Marys tumbling
from your lips. Shoulders
already bearing the weight.

You look only once,
then take a seat nearby.
Mice scuttle in the hay,
brittle leaves scratch
in the autumn chill.

Back at home you place
the mother-of-pearl
rosary in your wife's
hand as she sleeps.
She sits up. She knows.

emily f. kerlin

Imagined Mercy

behind the old train depot
    there's a path to a small creek
        where a person might find a broken flip-flop or an empty fifth

but this evening it was a blue
    towel, half-wet on the rocky bank
        not yet pulled into the slow winter currents

the other part waving in the icy water
    covering and uncovering the tender shape
        of a tabby, its fur like the flash of a shy fish

and the small stone stair
    where you yourself would sit
        if it was you, holding her under

until she stilled
    in her soft blue shroud
        and floated gently into the black

Your First Apartment

We climbed the stairs
together to number 3
where the landlord
fiddled key in lock
to let us into a musty room
with the shabby couch,
dirty overhead light
and pint-sized stove,

and though my house
is less than a mile
away, and though
your room there
is free, just like
the food is free
and the parking
and the wi-fi
and the heating
and the laundry–
all free,

you look around
this tiny place
and know
what you want–
which is to live
on your own,
here in this room

emily f. kerlin

over the cafe
with the dawn-
facing window,
where paint chips fall
in the dusty sill
and clinks of spoons
in coffee cups
trail up the vents
instead of heat,

you know now
as well as you knew
that day in the hospital
twenty years ago
that it was time
to take your leave
of me

and with the same,
sudden flexing
of your gentle,
sturdy will, you show
me how you find
your own way

and carefully,
carefully, without
stumbling down
these stairs, this
is how I let you.

Quarrel With the Sky

My pushmower is a loud,
toothy monster on a leash.

I zig-zag it around the lawn
to avoid a bunny, dwarfed by the grass.

He hops around me. Only the tips
of his pink ears give him away.

After the last swath, I kill the motor.
He scampers off in the still air,

lengthwise across the yard.
I exhale relief, then stop,

as a red-shouldered hawk drops in
to claw the screeching white fluff

above the maple leaves. Sunlight
cuts through the branches

onto his mama, her body taut, eyes
locked in a quarrel with the sky.

Nothing Between Them

it was Fort Benning
for officer training camp
and dozens
of US Army-
censored letters

it was the Atlantic
the European theater

it was men that needed
him more than she

it was the Jeeps
needing a good mechanic

it was five years
of worry and newspaper
clippings

it was the long way
back
to the farm

it was the shy they felt
when he arrived,
his beard, strange
and untrimmed

it was the memory
of the ambush

it was the ambush
of memory

it was the baby,
colicky all night

it was chores

it was late nights grading
term papers
it was the children

it was the heat
it was the milking
it was the shelling
of peas

and black walnuts
it was the mowing
it was the canning
it was the mending
it was the snow drifting

over the road

it was the children

emily f. kerlin

and then, when
the children had grown,
it was his lungs,
and the constant problem
of breath

it was blood sugar dips
that had him anxiously
fishing his pocket
for a butterscotch

it was the black
that began in the toes
and rose like flood water

it was the chair she wheeled
him in to the bathroom
to draw a hot sink

it was the steam
clouding the mirror

it was the washcloth
she'd wrung for him

it was his hands
pressing the warmth to his face
for a few blissful minutes
until it cooled

The Viral Remedy

No one could predict this
savage theft of our comings
and goings by the red-wreathed
corona, mercilessly linking bat
to civet to fragile lace of human lung,

but here we are, one year later, stooped
over stoves, holding navel oranges to flame,
mashing the charred fruit
with sugar, spooning it warm
into our mouths like we are
our own mothers.

The Wind Across the Ocean

for Thomas

think of your first time
on Rodeo Drive
hunting for cheap Docs,
a Telecaster,
some bootleg Pixies,
stonewashed Levis

when a bullet pop,
quick crumple and slow
sprawl of a young man
played out like a low-
budget film sequence

the Santa Ana winds
carried sirens as paramedics
rushed to the scene
outside the Thai place
where you were learning
to eat fiery soup,
sharp barbs of pepper
cutting your mouth

you were just a blue-
eyed boy then, thirty
years shy of the man
you are now: less blue
less blonde, writing all

your songs in English,
the shape now of your
toughened tongue

far from the quiet
place across the sea
where your sweet mother
simmers potatoes
on a stove and cool
ocean breezes still
blow across your bed

The Summer Widower

I worry about the man
on the corner. He's not home
much, but evenings I see
his bald head in the window,
still as a lamp for hours.

Tomorrow, I'll bring him a bowl
of tomatoes and take a shovel
to save his wife's flower garden
from the advancing pokeberry,
thistle and voracious slugs.

For now, a skinny tomcat
peers out from the darkened porch.
Spiders lace up the front door
and light peers over
his softly sloping shoulders.

A late summer's breath
ushers the swing to do what it did
years ago. It shifts the curtains
in the sill. Pushing them out.
Pulling them in.

Old Friend

Hear you're in town. Lie awake,
thumb something quick. Play with syntax,
tone, blame but it's still not right. See
your lovely face, vomit falling
softly off one cheek, your red nose
the telltale sign of sliding off
your slippery wagon. Settle
on *hey. Dinner if u promise*
not 2 pass out before dessert.

      Later,
at a quiet table in back
you drop off into your 80-
proof stupor. Pull out a folded-
up poem in microscopic
purple gel pen which I've carried,
along with other small fragile
artifacts: the Nina Simone
mix-tape, a small wax Buddha and
my love, which has flown off
into the night like a flop-winged bat.

A Winter in Montana

Up near Whitefish
thousands of migrating
snow geese touched down
in poisoned waters and perished,
every one. White feathers
undulated under
November clouds.

That New Year's Eve
Kent from the dishroom,
and from Nebraska before that,
set a martini in front of me,
then leaned in under the stuffed moose
for something in return.
Even my boyfriend laughed
because the poor guy was just drunk.

Later Kent went out
to the machine shed,
–where the stink of two-stroke
engines may have taken him back
to a sunny midwestern lawn,
kneeling over a mower with his dad–
and in that cold, lonely sanctuary
of early morning,
he nudged a gun
to his temple

while the rest of us
slept off hangovers:
the sous chef,
saving up for culinary school,
the busboy snowboarder,
trying to snag sponsorship,
the bartender working his way
back home to Brazil.

We woke to the sound
of a Blackfeet woman
pounding the first white cross
of the year next to the highway,
under a silent sky, waiting
for life to return.

The First Marriage

I.

On the way home from O'Hare
when my mom was nineteen
and freshly back from a year
in Stockholm, she lit a menthol in the back
seat of Grandpa's Chevy and lobbed
a grenade into the front bench seat:
she was running off
with the Mitchell kid,
even though he wasn't quite
discharged from the service,
there was just one place to go:
west. To Eugene; as in Oregon;
as in the furthest away
from Jo Daviess County
you could drive
without putting that pretty
little MG in the Pacific

II.

which is exactly what Grandpa
recommended she do and, for once,
she listened. Somewhere there is a picture
of her in white carrying a bouquet,
cheeked up to a man
with curly hair and a smirk
so I guess there was a wedding
but no one was there, the dress

and the gold band are long gone,
and no one knows how
they cobbled jobs or learned
to make meatloaf. How he came home
with hands that wouldn't scrub clean.
How she had to wear heels and hose
and applish lipstick. How proud
they must have been
when they put a down payment
on a little place along the Lorane Highway.
They played house and painted
a nursery pink until Mom's appendix
popped like a birthday balloon
and that brought it all to a full
stop.

III.
They buried that
little girl in a small box
on a hill. But before
the grass grew over
her, he fell to their bathroom
floor, too heavy to catch.
She had been cleaning
the bathtub, Comet on her hands,
arms wet. The paramedics
were late, and no one guessed
from his face how the blood circled
already in his skull,
the maelstrom in his brain.

emily f. kerlin

When he came home
from the hospital he was so mean
even the greasy shop guys
didn't want him.

IV.
When you're twenty-two
you figure you can begin again
so she drove the MG back across
the Rockies alone with her cat
and a case of Kools and no idea
that she would see him next
at his wake. The papers said pushers
shot him up and burned down
that little bungalow in the valley,
where smoke settled
into their collective choke.

House Fire

The Dominican sisters,
having finished vespers, are quiet;
the convent dark.

Just down the road a curly-haired
man sits in an old foursquare and works
out chords for a James Taylor tune.

He stops now and then
to fill the belly of the Fisher
with wood he split that afternoon.

He's likely a good beer or two
into that night alone with the kids,
dirty dinner dishes languishing

in the enamel sink, waiting,
like the rest of the house,
for her return on Tuesday.

The room is warm. He sings
Handyman soft,
so it won't carry upstairs.

Out back Fever River flows
slow through timber, deep
under midwinter ice.

emily f. kerlin

Perhaps he glances up, scratching
his whiskers or maybe when he tips
his beer back, he spies those

sly flames ripping up
the lath and plaster
like predator on prey.

One minute later,
memory's scroll commences
with the smell of smoke

and panic as he burst into our room
to yank us from our beds,
to shove our arms into coat sleeves.

We are football-carried down
the stairs and into the black
shower of falling ash.

I am given the mittened hand of my brother
and in the other he loops the leash
of our jumpy Chesapeake.

We three stand on the gravel shoulder
next to the rural route box with firm
orders: Don't. Move.

I don't remember the fire trucks,
only the wait. Watching my father
run back in for his guitar.

The Great Grandmothers

They called it Spanish Lady and whispered the name
while pulling fat hornworms off the tomatoes.

They pruned potato vines, then waited two weeks to dig
them up; in that time another neighbor was gone, or a cousin.

In tidy kitchens they sewed silk pouches filled with camphor
and hung them around the soft, small necks of our grandparents.

They made blood omelets and bone broth from the old hen.
Wrapped the beaks and feathers in newspaper for the burn pile.

The grim headlines turned to ash and floated up into the bright sky.
Look to them, I'm telling you. It's not Spanish Lady, but it is not different.

Think of how they pushed through -- lovely, even in their fear,
like the crocuses pushing purple into this cold March morning.

Coming of Age

In Edgar County
boys speed by on tar and chip

without slowing for black ice
or hairpin turns.

Guardrails wink
in the winter sun like a tease.

On this morning
there is a sharp yelp

from old Gunnar before he
limps off to die in the ditch.

The old man hears it,
heads down to the road,

looks at the bloodied fur
and hollers for his son.

Too cold for shovelin, better
take 'im up to the burn pile.

Gives him a gallon of gas
and a box of matches.

Later, at his desk,
the boy's fingers are numb

and dirty. His clothes
reek of smoke.

There's a hardness
in his belly

and an awful urge
to cry.

Euphemism

When I say he's gone
or that he passed away
it's not that I can't see
him on the hospital bed
after all the beeps
and pumps were stopped,
lying still as the shadow
of the house we loved
each other in.

Believe me when I say
I'm not avoiding the D-word–
I only mean to set this apart
from the other Dead things
I've known like cell phones,
opossums and houseplants,
which haven't left me
feeling like I have also
crossed over.

Ditch Bag

Maybe an envelope of old
photos, a notebook,
the red sweater,
my vitamins. We talk

a lot about democracy
like it's a flat stone
skipped across
the water,

how no one thought
it could work and also
how everyone knows
how to save it.

I grew up thinking a lot
about nuclear war
but that's an old worry now,
polished up and put away.

Last night I saw two eyes
peering up from the storm sewer
and then, after I was sized
up as harmless enough,

four claws and a furry body
with a ringtail spilled
into the street. I guess he's been

emily f. kerlin

watching, plotting his next move

too. I add some snacks
to the ditch bag list,
for the critters. In the dark
we understand each other,

both feel the chill,
the cool water poured
over summer's embers.
Flowers gone, leaves flaming

out. Of the many deaths
that lead us into November
it's the morning sun
I miss the most

since I can no longer fill the dark
hours with sleep. At night
new worries and heartaches
spill over their banks.

Do you know they are putting
another coal mine
on another river?
Because that's what addicts do:

pillage the beauty
they can no longer see.

I add poster board
and Sharpies to my list.

How am I just now
realizing that the things I love
are too many and far too heavy
on the shoulders.

A Farewell to Loneliness

You don't mind a little coontail corded around your ankles,

                                                        do you?

Or ribbon leeches,

                  passing gently   over the tops of your feet?

Do you hear it?

                  There is a loon calling,

                                    but not for you.

You are alone   with a quarter moon.

                        It is more   than enough.

A spill of starlight moves   across the sky.

You shed your clothes;

          your body slides easily   into the dark,

              your arms rise

                    until you are wearing   the lake.

If someone appeared

right now   --*anyone*--

you could certainly fall   in love.

But there is just you.   The lady of the lake.

Tell me   have you ever loved

anything more?

ACKNOWLEDGMENTS

With gratitude to my loving family and my many mentors from the Glass Room Poets & Quintessential Poets

"Fourth of July" appeared in the November 2019 issue of *Bridge*.

"Christmas Eve" appeared in the January 2020 issue of *Cider Press Review.*

"House Fire" appeared in the July 2020 issue of *Storm Cellar.*

"Farewell to Loneliness" appeared under the title "Lady of the Lake" in the July 2020 issue of *Blue Mountain Review.*

"The Golden Boy Goes on Hospice" and "The Summer Widower" appeared in the Fall 2020 issue of *Pittsburgh Poetry Journal.*

"The Great Grandmothers" appeared in the Spring 2022 issue of *Split Rock Review.*

"Imagined Mercy" appeared in the Spring 2023 issue of *The MacGuffin.*

"Your First Apartment" appeared in the Spring 2023 issue of *Sheila-Na-Gig.*

"Old Friend" appeared in the February 2022 issue of the *Cider Press Review,* under the title, "The Apology".

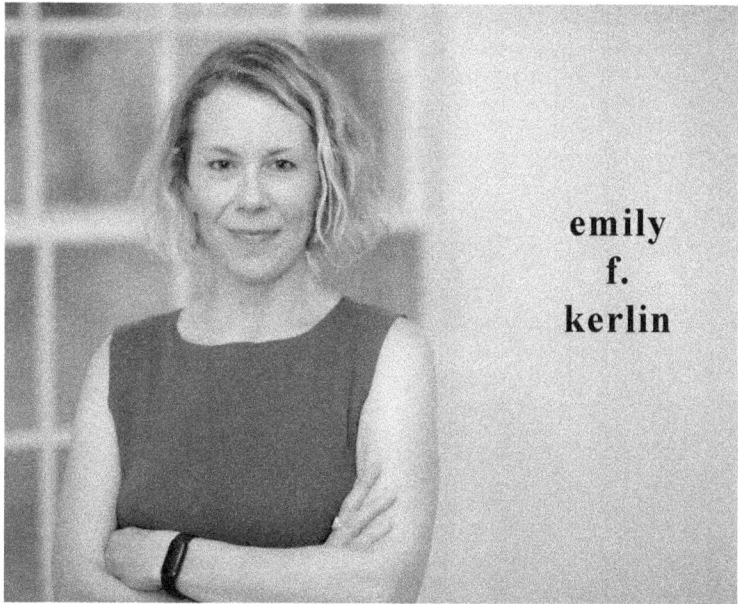

**emily
f.
kerlin**

Emily F. Kerlin has called the following things home: a 13-tatami-mat flat in Japan, a gaff-rigged schooner in Manhattan, a stone home on an island in Lake Michigan, a blue left-zip mummy bag in British Columbia, a Guatemalan trimaran in Micronesia, a ski lodge in Montana and a small town near the Baltic coast of Germany. Her current home sits at 728 feet above sea level in Urbana, Illinois where she has been teaching the difference between "chicken" and "kitchen" to English language learners in public schools for the last 20 years. She has published poems in *Sheila-Na-Gig, Bridge, Storm Cellar, The Pittsburg Poetry Journal, The MacGuffin, Split Rock Review* and *Blue Mountain Review.* You can find her at emilykerlin.com